WRITING MATTERS AND SO DO YOU

Writing With A Mental Health Focus

Christina Vourcos

To my writing community, thank you for being there for me and continue to be.

EPISODE 1: WHAT WORKS FOR ME MIGHT NOT ALWAYS WORK FOR YOU

Before I started my indie author journey, and as I moved forward, I found myself reading a lot of writing craft books. It was my way of figuring out how everyone else took the writing process. I've had college and graduate school classes focused on creative writing that provided the foundation I needed, but I needed more. I wanted to write a novel that was worth publishing. It was something that I had to figure out through my research and practice. I had to switch my focus from writing as a hobby to a career. It took a lot of effort and a realization that I could do it and had to make it my own. There's no one solution.

I hope to provide what we need to do as a writing community that will allow us to become better writers moving forward and help the writers start. No one said anything we care deeply about would be easy, but we do need to ensure that we take care of ourselves as best as possible. If we don't, we will lead to burnout. I've had it at least twice in my life and continue to work on recovering from it and preventing the possibility of burnout. Let's make this clear. I'm not referring to procrastination because that's when you don't want to do something. It's not writer's block because you might know what you want to write. Sometimes, even when you want to write and know what you want to write, you can't find the path to write. It's when we should stop and figure out what to do.

We have to include self-care when we talk about the writing process, revising, editing, marketing, and all the aspects of what we do to make sure our work is the best it can be and available to our readers. We're all different writers. Each path will only work for some. We must accept and support all writers in their path wherever it leads them. We have to figure out what we can do moving forward. That can be letting go of what we can't control and focusing on what we can. It can be a struggle. We have to admit that not only to ourselves but to others. We're all human. The only way others will be able to understand and feel understood is if we share our struggles when we can. I don't mind discussing mental health and how it impacts all aspects of our lives, including our writing.

We must reflect to discover what we can do because we need superpowers. Even Kara Danvers (aka Supergirl) struggles to get everything done. It's time to focus on what works with writing, marketing (including social media), and taking care of your health (including mental health). It's about the small steps forward. It can be challenging because we have high expectations put on us, as well as high expectations for ourselves. I know that I have both. Sometimes, we must let others know they add pressure, even when well intended. We have to remind ourselves that rest is just as important as progress.

There's so much writing advice. One is about writing every day, even if you don't feel like it. It's the wrong perspective. Yes, you might have a deadline, but if you don't find time to take care of yourself or journal before you complete what you need to do. It will make things so much harder. We have to reevaluate what we're doing, especially if we're working part-time. I continue to do this because I'm not a full-time author (as much as I wish I could be). We have to find ways to make things easier for ourselves. Sometimes, that means less is more. Everywhere around us, we might find a message that makes us feel guilty that we're not doing enough. At what point is enough?

We have to keep learning. I love learning, so it makes some

things easier for me. Learning is the only way that we can grow and improve. That's what we want to do as authors no matter our path. I found some of the best things happen when you take risks. You still think things through, but leaping into the unknown may lead you to amazing places. You might have been told never to quit. It's incorrect. We must strategically quit things that don't work to find what to do. We've learned sometimes the hard way, especially during the COVID-19 pandemic, that the future is a learning curve. We are still determining what will happen. All we can do is focus on what are our strengths and find those who can support us. Because it's true, "Teamwork makes the dream work." Let's get started.

EPISODE 2: WRITERS NEED SELF-CARE

Writers, we need self-care. You might think it's an activity that indulges in something you don't normally do, such as having something sweet. As someone who has been brought up with the idea of indulging oneself as a negative thing, it can sometimes be tough to do. I've realized that I've learned it all wrong. We need to take care of ourselves first before we can help others. It's much like when they tell you to put on an oxygen mask before helping others with it in case of an emergency in an airplane. Self-care is that urgent, too. Imagine waking up with a fully charged battery, and throughout the day, you're losing that charge. If you don't recharge (aka self-care), you'll run low or even power off (aka burnout). It usually takes much longer for you to get to burnout, but some get closer each day because of everything we do. As writers, we try to complete all that we can each day. Now, it's beyond writing each day. We also have to work on editing, making sure everything is ready for publication, we have to promote, and doing additional activities to get the word out that our work is available. Plus, if it's not our full-time job, we have another job that we have an additional to-do list to complete. Some of us must take care of family and all that comes with that. Then, in 2020, we added the COVID-19 pandemic to that mix. At first, we didn't know what to do, and now we do, but we still struggle to figure out the best ways forward. No wonder we're all stressed out.

Self-care is about finding time for ourselves that will help replenish our energy and, most importantly, our creativity by doing things that will make us happy. It can be hard to carve out a self-care routine for the week or even each day when we're constantly told that we need to be doing something productive all the time. Recently, I've seen a trend of people sharing their top procrastination techniques on social media. While it may have started as a way to lead writers to focus more on their writing and a critique on social media for taking time away from us, I saw it as something much worse. Instead of making it something relatable for writers, it's making writers feel guilty. Some might say, good. They shouldn't be on social media as they should be writing, but that's wrong. There's usually a reason why we're on social media.

First, as a writer, we need to use social media to share what we're working on and what we have available and find ways to connect to readers along with others. Second, our need to be social goes beyond online; we humans are social creatures. When we can't interact with others near us, we will find different ways to interact with others, including with technology. We don't see it that way, but it's actually a need for us to be social. Third, and finally, we use social media to express ourselves and provide an outlet to destress. Even good things come with negatives; we have to check in to see if we're finding value in what we're exploring on the internet. If not, we must take a break and find another avenue to help us. The most important thing to focus on is that we need to permit ourselves to relax. It is okay to take time to relax. You aren't being lazy. We can't work 24/7. We have our limits. Rest allows us to refuel our batteries.

When we work on self-care, we can improve our physical and mental health. Especially with mental health, self-care can manage stress, lowering your risk for illnesses and increasing your energy. While I recommend finding resources if you're struggling a lot with your mental health, such as using the new emergency number 988 or finding affordable local therapy options, self-care can help us deal with our everyday struggles and crises. According to Mental Health First Aid USA, it's been clinically proven that a self-care routine can reduce anxiety and depression, reduce stress, and much more. We're able to adapt when changes occur and recover from setbacks. Self-care can actually produce increased productivity.

As I've brought up on social media about mental health (my way to break the stigma about discussing mental health), if we run trying to get everything done at a high pace, we will head to burnout. I've experienced at least two instances of burnout. The first affected my job in the worst way imaginable. I was so burnt out that I had to leave my job. It still upsets me to this day that people could see the signs, but they took it as usual for someone starting in the education profession. I knew something was wrong, but I kept pushing until my breaking point because I didn't have what I needed to take care of myself. Reimagining the education system is something that we need to do, but let's not get off-topic. The second time, I had to be told that I was dealing with burnout because even though I had experienced similar symptoms before, I wasn't at the same stressful breaking point as the first. This time, I knew more about caring for my mental health. You know why I didn't really notice because I was still doing everything I could do.

I want to do my best as a part-time educator, author, and volunteer on a notable website. It takes a lot of "hats" to make all that happen. I'm doing several things in every area. Now, I must find ways to check in with myself, especially when I can't speak to my counselor. Am I doing everything to take care of myself physically and mentally? They both interconnect a lot, too. So what if you focus so much on a project and forget to have lunch, you'll be running low later and possibly not getting what you need. I've found a lot of writers finding their ways to make self-care a priority. It still needs to be focused on more. We can only run on empty because our work will struggle. Some things I've seen are planning out their day on when they will get writing done or when they will do it during the week. Some focus on planning everything they do as best as possible while being flexible. Others try to find time to exercise before they write or find something they enjoy doing scheduled. Some use the Pomodoro technique to write in short sprints with scheduled breaks. In some cases, they are doing the check-in to see how they are doing. Self-care can focus more on getting better sleep, scheduled meditation, or evaluating your expectations. It could be journaling our thoughts. It might be a strange suggestion to writers when we write all the time, but sometimes, we get so focused on producing something for others that we forget about ourselves. That can sometimes lead to difficulty in making progress on our creative projects. It's all about finding what works best for you. You must try things out for yourself and see how they impact you. Sometimes, that can change over time; you might have to find new things to focus on.

Even this nonfiction is my way of sharing what I'm passionate about and helping others and a way of self-care. I've been struggling with my creative writing. Being able to write something different gives me a chance to shift gears to recharge my creativity. I hope this will help you and me focus on our mental health, including self-care, and lead us back to productivity with our projects. For me, my serial fiction. My writing matters to me because I want to do all I can to complete it for my readers, but I also need to take care of myself. Now I'm going to get a drink of water. I'm a bit behind on my daily water. Did you know the lack of water can affect our mental health and creativity? It's true.

EPISODE 3: WE NEED TO ACCEPT WE'RE ALL DIFFERENT WRITERS

The reason why not all writing books work for us is that we're different. We all have to find what works for us, but we must also realize that we all come from different perspectives. This is something that we have to keep in mind when we write, as well as focus on our mental health.

We all come from different backgrounds, some more diverse than others. When we reach out to discuss our cultures and the different parts that make up our communities, we find opportunities to address our struggles and strengths. I'm thankful to be a Greek Latina. Even exploring my cultures, I realize how multigenerational aspects have led us to need to focus more on our feelings. I'm thankful that my generation and other generations are working towards making changes. It takes time to realize what we can do to improve and make that happen. Knowing that my Latinx community is diverse makes it even more important to see different perspectives within. It's a strength that we have. We're getting more opportunities to share how diverse our community is than what was done before in different writing mediums. It can be a struggle to hold the weight of the expectations of others. We have to do it right all the time. Even then, we forget that all we can do is do our best from our perspective and what we can learn to grow our perspective for the future.

Regarding mental health, we can forget that we all deal with different life stressors. That's why we must do our best to find ways to take care of our physical and mental health, as they're connected. You know what you need, but sometimes you don't. That's where you want to get the help you need to be able to keep moving forward. Even when you're physically sick, it affects your mental health. It drains your body from being able to function correctly. You can get depressed and more anxious than normal. It doesn't help that we always run with the idea of productivity as valuable. In some cases, we're not able to take a day off to rest because of a loss of pay, and even if we can, we feel like we're good enough because we're not able to get what we need and want to be done. On the days when I'm sick, not only do I feel bad physically, but I've had moments where I'm upset because now I'm going to be behind.

I've had to work on dealing with this through counseling sessions and just personally working on accepting that rest is valuable. The sickness can go beyond the common cold. As I've mentioned before, I've had burnout, which can turn into physical symptoms of fatigue, brain fog, and body aches. Even the overall stress of COVID-19 has led to these symptoms. At first, I worried it was COVID-19, but the more I dealt with my health, the more I realized that my body was affected by more than illness. Some have long-COVID or Chronic Fatigue Syndrome, which they must deal with daily. We still don't have enough treatments to deal with these. These steps are similar: organizing the day, finding moments to rest to recharge, and learning when you have the most energy. It's deciding what is the most important thing to do and when. It isn't easy when we have deadlines looming.

We have those dealing with different mental illnesses beyond depression and anxiety. We have those who must figure out different ways to live with their disabilities. Especially when those who can aren't willing or have time to think of them when doing everyday activities. In some cases, we haven't learned enough to understand and respond in the best way possible fully. It's something that we all have to work on. As an educator, I've learned that it's more important to be equitable than equal in instruction. It's something that education still needs to work on, but it's an important focus. We have to find what is best for each person because, just like writers, learners (including us) have a different style that works for them to learn.

We might be visual, auditory, kinesthetic, and reading/ writing. As writers, we have different styles, not just in the words we write but also in our writing, editing, revising, and publishing methods. Some plan, some are intuitive, and some are a blend of both. It might be even more than that. We might have a different style per step in the writing process; we might change our style each day. We have different situations. We have different publishing paths: traditional, hybrid, and indie (small pub or self-pub). Some writers even go towards other paths: TV, movies, and theater. Even songwriting. Or a mix of these. Depending on those paths, you might have different things you need to do to get your work published and available for readers or different hurdles to reach audiences. No matter what direction you go, there's not an easy journey, no matter what people say. We have to focus on why we decided to publish.

We all need to accept that we're different, which is good. We must accept that we all have different paths and ways to succeed. We must only accept when our work and worth are valued, as well as the work and worth of others, especially those who haven't had the opportunities in the past because of discrimination or how the system was built. It's time to work together to support one another so all our writing and voices matter while being respectfully critical of where we need to improve. We can do this in every aspect of our lives, from social media, events, interactions, work opportunities, and writing. We need to learn about how the systems of our society have been put in place to make changes.

EPISODE 4: WHAT CAN WE DO MOVING FORWARD?

That's the question, isn't it? That might be the reason why you decided to read this nonfiction. Let's look at the steps forward to ensure we focus on mental health while writing and doing everything we do as writers. I say writers because being a writer goes beyond being a published author. We all need to find what works for our path. Some things can be done for all kinds of writers.

A notable one is scheduling check-ins for mental health and physical health throughout the day and weekly. It's something we might ask someone else (if we don't, maybe you should), but also for ourselves. You might do it already when you feel weird or not well. It can be frustrating when you need to know what is wrong. The more that we schedule this time into our lives, the better. We can catch things we might not otherwise do or help ourselves move forward. I know it's something I'm still working on. It can also be tough to explain how you feel, including physically. So, we need to listen to our bodies by doing a quick body scan. Am I tired? Why might I feel tired? What do I need to do to feel better? Does my body hurt? If it does, it might affect my brain as nerve sensors are connected to the brain. If you can't focus, how can you write? Are you eating balanced meals? Do you need a snack while writing? Are you drinking enough water? Do you feel sick? What symptoms can you notice? Are you dressed for success? It could get overwhelming once we start to think of these questions. That is why it can be helpful to journal when you can, daily or weekly.

Find what your stressor would be. If you're feeling something, what are you doing? What were you thinking about? Has anything changed in your life? What has taken over your time and mental energy? That's right. We use mental energy when we go through different ideas and multiple decisions and when we're creative. How has work been? Is your work life mixing with your home life? Do you need balance? It's all essential questions to ponder. Name your feelings; writing them down can make the action stronger. Sometimes, we must move our bodies around to get unstuck or feel what we feel. It's like those Grey's Anatomy scenes where Meredith and others turn on music and just dance it out. We might need some social interaction, too. See what works for you on this part. Find something you enjoy until you feel more motivated. Something with our physical environment might be throwing us off. Do you ever feel like cleaning when you need to write? You might think it's a procrastination technique to delay writing, but it is what you need to declutter your mind to write. In other aspects, some of us might need more energy to do the necessary cleaning. Is there someone who can help? What if you do a bit at a time? Some might feel like clutter helps, but you'll have to clean at some point.

After you journal your thoughts, focus on how you can plan your week or your days. Become a scientist by figuring out what day works best for you. Or if several days of the writing process work. Schedule when you'll write when you'll fill your creative well, and what you need to do to rest. Sometimes, the moments away from your writing can lead to exciting breakthroughs. This can be done well with a planner. Even if you don't plan too much (even with your writing), having something written down somewhere about when would be best to get writing done and everything else will be helpful for you. Plus, you'll unload your mind by not worrying about what you need to remember. Writing isn't all that we do; we also create content for our social media to attract and interact with readers, we figure out what marketing strategies might work, we might have another job that we work on, and our own lives to experience. It's a lot that we're taking on.

Check to see if you can find affordable counseling services near you. If not, consider contacting 988 and see if they can provide direction on how to help. Having someone to springboard what you're dealing with can help a lot. Sometimes, it helps to focus more on your writing. They can help you create the goals you want to achieve and the steps you need to attain them. I'm thankful to find local affordable counseling services (they're remote with Zoom). Besides counseling, you can find others in the writing community with whom you can springboard your ideas. They can be your Watson to your Sherlock as you figure out the mystery of your writing.

As mentioned earlier, make sure you have a healthy diet. I've found a primarily Mediterranean diet helps me, but I can also find healthy ways to make Mexican food. This way, I can have both of my cultures' food while caring for my body. It also helps to get some exercise there too. I used to be better at it, but I need to get back to being more regular about exercising. It doesn't have to be running around the block. Make sure you keep a good sleep schedule. When I don't, it really throws me off all day. It's better to be best rested so you can write and be productive than not. That's why figuring out when and what works to take necessary breaks. You shouldn't be worried about writing while you're taking a break. Even watching a good TV show episode or movie can bring you the inspiration you need. Distract you from your worries for a bit. That invisible plate includes all that you should be doing. Throw it to the ground and say, "Opa!"

Most of all, we need to speak out about our struggles. It's also when you can because it can be tough to share. This can help you process what you've dealt with and what you can do moving forward, but it can also help others realize that they have similar struggles. It's a good way to support our writing community and lend an understanding perspective when listening to others. We have a wonderful writing community, especially in the Kindle Vella author community. We celebrate our successes and motivate each other when we struggle with writing, editing, publishing, marketing, etc. This nonfiction can help my writing community to continue to thrive. It can be challenging, especially as an indie author and Kindle Vella author, because we need to be constantly productive in releasing new episodes and books while maintaining our social media and marketing our work with everything else. If we make these steps, we can make strides forward.

ocuses on personal branding) and Jenn DePaula (who focuses on Book Marketing for authors). I found myself finding what I enjoyed best from them and creating my version. Knowing what steps I need to take daily and weekly toward achieving my goals allows me to focus on what I can control. Especially when so much of our lives, including our careers, is out of our control, even for indie authors.

We can get focused on trying to get a certain number of reads, followers, and royalties coming in. While this can be helpful at times to see how we're growing and reaching more readers, as well as handling our finances, it can start to become all that we do to reach some unattainable goal each month. I get it. We want to do our best and get a chance to reach readers and get a good bonus. I feel the same way. I also struggle to continue as an indie author, but I'm thankful each month for the opportunity to keep going with what is offered and the support given to me and my writing. At the same time, our writing career is unpredictable. We can never really know how well we will do each month. This is difficult, especially for those who are trying to get by. We might put all of our extra funds, effort, and passion into it, and we don't know if it will get a return. That's why we must focus on what we can do. Do your best to get writing (as well as revising and editing) done weekly as much as possible, find your schedule for promoting your work, set up ads that you can check occasionally, and connect with others when you can. Plus, reading and refilling your creativity well. If you're on the indie author track, you might also be adding formatting your books for standard formats to publish. This can also be a shift for those who started with Kindle Vella to publish into standard formats 30 days after completing a season or a serial.

If you know me, I tend towards perfectionism. So, it is no wonder some of my anxiety is rooted in that. Some of it is how I grew up with the demand to be at my best and slightly over-concerned parents, but it's also aspects at school, work, and now my career. I want to show the best I can be when I can. It can be frustrating when I put a lot of effort into something

EPISODE 5: ACCEPT WHAT YOU CAN'T CHANGE, FOCUS ON WHAT YOU CAN

As I got started as an indie author, I was trying t[o] up everything that I could that would set me up for su[c] Sometimes, I spread myself too thin, focusing on minor stuff setting up a merch shop) when I needed to focus on what [c] attract readers to read what I had published or something else could help me move forward. I'm not saying those minor th[ings] aren't necessary, but not in the early stages, especially if y[ou] starting Kindle Vella. While I feel more set up now that I focus more on my writing, publishing, and engaging with rea[ders] through Kindle Vella, my newsletter, and social media, it r[eally] took some time to figure it out, and I'm still working on it. I [have] been on the right path since the start of Kindle Vella in July 2[0]

In the next month, August 2021, I began my start [with] publishing on Kindle Vella, but also as an indie author. I [was] not only trying to figure out the platform like many fel[low] authors, including some experienced authors but also learr[ning] how to create an author brand. I got some inspiration fr[om] fellow authors, including Kindle Vella, like Christina Farley, B[...] Revis, and LaShaunda Hoffman, who has a fantastic nonfict[ion] Kindle Vella about Building Your Readership. I've read books [and] got inspiration from social media experts like Karen Happel (w[...]

and then realize I still need to catch something. I must remind myself that even those with many resources still have struggles and errors in their manuscripts, no matter how much they were overlooked. We're all human. While I've realized I must overcome these perfectionistic tendencies, it's still a work in progress (pun intended).

This can also be when we think we're not good enough or think that our work will never compare to others. We have to recognize these thoughts, observe how they affect us, and let them drift from us like a stream. Letting go of these thoughts isn't the same as ignoring or pushing the thoughts away. This process allows you to accept and move forward. Other aspects that you can do to overcome this can be writing down a list of ideas for later, writing a lot, especially in public; sometimes, it's best to wait to revise, being kind to yourself as you write, and going beyond the written process. At the same time, I wouldn't recommend writing every day (unless you need to or want to) as that can add additional pressure, finding time to write for yourself and others to give yourself some time to let your words flow. Be open to new things, learn from others, and seek positive support.

Sometimes, all you need to do is do a short meditation and journal before getting the writing you need or want to do. Another excellent option that I've learned recently is memory planning. It's a different approach to using your physical or digital planner. Lately, it's been my digital Passion Planner (to keep track of everything), my physical Paper Hearts Planner (to focus on planning my writing), and other resources, including the Beth Revis' Paper Hearts series. Memory planning goes beyond what we need to do in standard planning. It's a good way to focus on our mental health as well.

Memory planning is the process that allows us to remember different aspects of our daily lives, from things we do to how we're feeling, inspiration, or listing what we're grateful for. It can calm our anxiety. It's a process of reflection and can be a creative process. This can be done in a standard journal, but I found it interesting to see it being done in a planner where you can already have the set dates or undated ones where you can add. In this format, you can have a certain amount of space to put down your thoughts, lyrics, gratitude, highlights, lessons learned, a brain dump of your feelings or thoughts, or record memories you don't want to forget. The best part is you can decorate your planner for each day or weekly spread however you want and be inspired by what you place into your planner. With my digital planner, I've been getting digital stickers to make my planner more my own. I recommend it.

It's also important to be flexible. Only some things will work out that day or when you want. So be ready to make a change to reach where you want to go. I'll explain more about flexibility when you want to get everything done.

EPISODE 6: HOW DO I GET WRITING DONE?

Where do I begin when I start a new project? It usually changes over time, but this has worked for me lately. I start with a synopsis first. You're going to say, "What? You don't even have an idea yet." You can expand from there if you can think up an idea for creating a synopsis. 'Save the Cat: Writes A Novel' has a short synopsis template. It's several sentences for three paragraphs. Then, expand to provide a story area. A story area is what TV writers use to pitch a TV show. This can be very similar to the one-page synopsis.

The story area is more specific than just expanding the synopsis. It can be a valuable resource to go back to keep track of what the essence of your story is about. You start with a good logline. The sentence includes the hero or anti-hero (or even villain), the goal, the obstacle, and the stakes. Now you're like, but I don't even have an idea to start with! I would head to what you enjoy or want to write about. What are your strengths, and what could you improve? It's all at the start of the planning stage.

After the logline, start thinking about the cast of characters. You can explore more with Beth Revis' Fast Draft Workbook to delve into your cast and build your world. For now, we're getting a rough idea we can fine-tune later. Next, in this story area, look at your format/tone. Most of us on Kindle Vella will be focusing on serialization, and then we can share what we think we can compare our ideas from in books, movies, TV, and plays. It doesn't have to be exact, but it is something that can help you think about your story, and eventually, you might use that to help explain your story. Be careful; if you share, you must think about your audience. They might assume it is closer to the exact "comp title" (what you're comparing to). This has led to issues with authors looking like they are leading readers to a false idea of your story.

Also, it's essential to think about marketing even at this stage. I mean something other than fitting your story into what is currently available or what could sell, although money can be essential. It's really thinking about what you want to release to the world. What do you hope to accomplish? How will you share it online through social media and email newsletter? It might seem daunting and even early to think about it in the early stage or even if you've written a bit already. You have to remember what you have written if you have published and how that will work for your brand. We all have a brand with our work and how we present it. This is a good time to journal to think about all these steps, including your brand. I'll discuss this more.

Let's get back to the story area. Think about what kind of themes you might focus on for your story. You can return to this later if you don't know that yet. Just think of something universal that many people can connect to, especially your ideal reader or audience. Now, use the following few pages to focus on the story's plot: the beginning, middle, and end. This is where you can also explore possible genres you will work in. What is usually expected? Use this to springboard what you could do. Go back to those similar works you were thinking about to figure out what you want to do that is familiar but different. After that, start working on your outline with the 'Save the Cat' beats, determining the genre and what you want to do. You can use Beth's workbook to write a few sentences per chapter or, in our case, an episode. This is best done in pencil.

Or what I like to do is use a Google Sheet to create my outline with the beats, the episode descriptions, and anything else I want to keep track of. I like this aspect because I feel I can revise my outline more as I work and visually see the big picture. This setup helps me have a good structure, especially when I fast draft, which is necessary as a Kindle Vella author. We must quickly write an episode, edit, revise, and publish each week while promoting our work. Some of us might even do more episodes per week or other projects within or outside of Kindle Vella. It's all up to what we can do. Some might even write ahead or use writing we have done already. No matter the setup, we must give ourselves grace when we struggle to finish something. We have a good plan, but even our mental health can bring us down. You knew I would bring it up eventually.

It's tough when I know what I want to do, but I feel some weeks that I'm drained or extra busy, and it's harder to focus on the words to write and publish, no matter how much I want to do it. However, it does reassure me that I have a plan to go to and look at it. I know that I can do it because I've done it before. Even with this nonfiction, I have an outline that I use that I revise when needed. I also plan a lot, even my schedule for the week, including my social media posts. It makes me feel like I know what I will do, even if things change. I'm always open to changes, too, as well as inspiration. It is great that I've moved from writing a lot ahead of time to writing as I publish through Kindle Vella. It's where I can see what works and what I can improve for the standard formats. It also allows me to work out the story and allow readers to read and provide feedback. It's something that really empowers me.

I've tried different setups, but this is my favorite. It makes sense since my favorite authors and TV writers inspire it. Even this week, I've struggled to get the words for my current serial fiction. I took a pause and focused on this nonfiction. I sometimes have to try a different kind of writing to make some progress. Eventually, I got everything done, but the switch between fiction and nonfiction has been a good way to allow my mind to write what it can as much as possible while giving it rest as well. We all have a lot of stress in our lives. It affects us. We can also lead ourselves into burnout by doing too much. Our health, physically and mentally, can affect us. It can be tough to take care of ourselves when we have things we need and want to get done, what we have planned and set out to do. Let's reflect on what we can do.

EPISODE 7: DO I NEED TO DO EVERYTHING?

This is a trick question. Determining your situation, you might have someone who can help you with marketing your work or the means to make everything possible regarding publishing. In other cases, you might need to do more because you don't have the means. Either way, it's essential to remember that while we do need to do our best with our writing and letting others know about our work, we also need to take a step back when we take on too much or want to do more than we can.

It's easier said than done. I know this from my own experience. First, I had to learn that it was okay not to be productive always and that rest was a way to be effective. Now, it's finding ways to make sure that I balance what I need to do and what to do, along with rest. As an indie author and one who does Kindle Vella, I'm doing more on my own, but I appreciate as much support from readers and authors as they can.

I always want to do more than I can actually do. A lot of times, I compare myself to myself in the past. I used to be able to do more of this or more during this time. It's been some work to rewire myself to realize that things can't always be the same and that I'm doing different things. I have to focus on what I can do. Some with chronic health issues focus on the spoon theory, invented by Christine Miserandino, which is a way to explain to others how they have only a certain amount of energy to spend each day and help visualize how much we can do (removing spoons) and what self-care we can incorporate (add spoons).

I've come to deal with moments of depression, anxiety, brain fog, fatigue, and burnout. As well as other health issues. Sometimes, it's constant; sometimes, it comes in waves. These are things that people don't usually see, along with other disorders and disabilities, as they can be hard to diagnose, masked, or part of a spectrum of characteristics. It's important to remind you to find assistance where possible (there are affordable options when you search) because no matter how much I feel, I need to do everything, like Supergirl. Even she can't do it all.

It is something we have to fight for as well. Publishing can do more to help in the traditional area. Companies that help indie authors self-publish can, too. As well as those whom we work for outside of publishing. We need to speak up. Otherwise, we will lead ourselves to burnout or worse symptoms. We have to be activists for ourselves and others. When we can, lend a hand or a supportive action. We have to think about what we need and what others might need before we speak up so it can lead to clear discussions of ways to move forward. We must listen to others and ourselves to take the necessary actions to find the best solution.

We also have to remember that things will change. We can plan. Planning can help a lot, but it can still be thrown out the window when something external and especially internal happens. When we try to do it all, and the situation changes, we can be led to feel like we need to catch up or we'll never catch up. What do we do when a lot of it is on us? We need to do a lot, and we want to do a lot. Or even have moments when you don't want to do something(s) even though you usually do. What can we do?

It's something that we have to work on each day. We have to focus on our priorities, along with rest. We have to give ourselves grace when we don't get everything done. We must keep letting others know what we're dealing with so they can work with us. We need to keep finding strategies that could help us. We must let our readers know that things take a bit longer than expected if you can make or extend your deadlines. They'll realize that they aren't the only ones dealing with struggles. You never know. You might help a fellow author as well. I know that this nonfiction has already been.

The more we focus on what we need to function, the better we can be productive. Also, don't forget the basics too. If you're dehydrated (you usually are if you start to feel thirsty), you need to get more water. Rest also includes sleep (that can be tough as well for us writers). The more that we do can also affect these basic needs as well. Let's not forget those who menstruate. Our PMS symptoms can be more debilitating than others realize, even ourselves. We don't know how our mental health and physical health will be each day, especially those dealing with chronic issues. There are things we can do. It helps to remind ourselves.

I know I always need to. I want to be supportive all the time. I want to get everything done as best as possible. I want to write. I want to read. I want to do many things and everything I need to do. No matter how much I take care of myself and find different solutions, it's still a struggle. It's still frustrating to deal with, but having reminders from others (including the IDONTMIND mental health campaign and fellow authors) and personal reminders can help us get through. You need to realize how much you can make a difference.

Let's focus on caring for ourselves and helping others do the same. Let's reflect on what we have done and what we can do. Let us accept that we can't do everything as much as we want to all the time. Let's continue learning and find ways to benefit the best versions of ourselves and others. How do we do this while writing, editing, marketing, and life? The journey is long, my friends. Learn, do what you can, and rest. Always be thankful for another day that we can keep striving for our dreams.

For now, I'll be testing the spoon theory to see how it can impact my work-life balance. I will collect my data for a few weeks and see what deductions can be made. I will share what I come up with within this nonfiction, as well as other additional aspects that we can do to focus on our mental health as writers, especially as Kindle Vella and indie authors.

EPISODE 8: FIND WHAT WORKS WITH MARKETING

There is a difference between Marketing and Promotion, although they are very similar. Remember that when I talk about Marketing, I refer to the process of establishing yourself as a writer rather than the typical market for traditional. Every writer must find how to market their work to connect with others. It's something where we show who we are as writers and individuals and how that connects with our writing. Promotion is all about the sale. Sure, we all want to make a profit from our work, especially if we're struggling with finances, but we have to make sure that we only make some things feel like a sale. This process can take time to figure out and establish through social media, newsletter/mailing lists, and other avenues. Only some have assistance; even if they do, aspects are still necessary to connect with your audiences.

This can take time, effort, and energy from what you are already doing as a writer. Some might feel like it isn't their job to do it, but it is as important as writing. I'm thankful that I love learning, especially about marketing and creating a personal brand, and that it doesn't feel like a chore. It doesn't mean that it doesn't affect me to have another thing to do on my long list of things that I do (writing, editing, website manager, part-time academic advisor, and more). It's an additional area that we need to focus on mental health while we complete these marketing steps throughout each month. I've previously mentioned the spoon theory, which has helped me see where I am, in many cases, taking on more than I can my health can take, at least now. You know me. I want to do it all.

In many cases, I've pushed through health issues to make sure I can update on social media because at least I can make some kind of progress, especially when I'm not feeling well enough to write. When I say I don't feel well enough to write, I mean brain fog plus body aches. Sometimes, other illnesses weigh on me, or I have both. Even PMS has been shifting how I feel and how my mind responds. It's frustrating because I often have the time and can't be in the right setting to write. I'm not talking about a lack of inspiration, although sometimes that does happen. It's like my body wants me to slow down, even if I'm not running a marathon. Mentally, in many cases, we are. It's something that I've had to realize that my health isn't going to make things easy. It also doesn't help that I feel behind on learning about marketing as an author, as it wasn't explored enough in college and graduate school. I loved my college and graduate experiences, but a lot was missing in many areas, and, looking back on it, I would have loved to have had more time to explore.

There's a lot I've had to find on my own through my own research, reading, and connecting with others. I've found many others who have inspired me and taught me what I've learned so far, and I know they will continue to do so. You have to figure it out for yourself as you have your struggles and schedule. Here is what I've done, what I've figured out, and what I hope to do moving forward. It was very basic at the beginning of publishing, especially on Kindle Vella. All I could do was share screencaps and photos of devices, add some digital notations and video record aspects of the experience. I knew that wasn't enough. I went searching for a free version of a graphic app. I needed to know I could use it for what I wanted. Suddenly, it gave me the tools to create the graphics I wanted. It was the next step. I still felt it wasn't enough to help my writing get the needed traction. I wanted to learn more about what I could do to improve. I always do this for everything, as you can tell.

I began finding others to teach me about content buckets,

which are several topics you rotate throughout the week and the month. This gives a good structure for figuring out what you will share and allows you to be known for something. You find something about what your writing is about that you can talk about. For example, I focus on mental health and psychology with 'Never Forget.' So, I've talked about my struggles, the value of focusing on your mental health, my interest in psychology, etc. From there, I can bring something that can connect my story to be of value to someone else. Additionally, I can focus on creating entertaining, inspiring, educational, or persuasive content that brings that across. This makes it more interesting than saying they should read your work. Even sharing quotes and hooks can be limiting, too. Making a mix of these can provide more to share. So I finally thought I had the tools I needed.

Then bam! My health made things harder. I wanted to keep at the same pace, but I couldn't. I didn't know what I could do. I didn't want to provide something that wasn't good enough for others, from my writing to my posts. That's not even discussing my newsletter (which I love, but it can take time to release). So I went searching again. I tried out different ideas for low-energy type posts. Something that wouldn't take so long to figure out would create or drain me in the process of showing up. It all comes down to the popular phrase, "Keep it simple." I noticed that I could incorporate myself with voiceover with a video or just a photo or video of myself (sometimes with a book) as a way to show myself without getting too involved. I'm not saying that I won't do videos where I chat, but I'm trying to spread those out more. Even with the graphics, focusing on simple and effective graphics rather than something elaborate. This provides me with more energy and creativity for my writing.

I will continue to figure things out and improve. I understand that and expect that because there always will be things that will change, and we have to learn to adapt. You can only achieve what you want when you keep striving to be your best. It's okay that you're still figuring it out. Keep learning, get inspired, and take the steps forward. Don't let one day of low views affect you. Look at the overall growth. I love that I will always be a forever learner. It's something that gives me the opportunities that I have.

EPISODE 9: IT'S OKAY IF YOU DON'T WRITE EVERYDAY

This might be shocking to some, especially in November, to say. You don't have to write every day. You can think about your writing and work on projects each day; it isn't necessary if you can write each day. The most crucial part is that you have a schedule (and flexibility for what life gives you) to keep you writing. The reason I bring this up is that as amazing as the National Novel Writing Month (NaNoWriMo) challenge is. Staying on track with the word count each day can be stressful. This stress can impact our mental and physical health. Additionally, many writers have suggested that writing each day is necessary. This can cause you to worry that you aren't doing enough. If you need to make some process each day, let me tell you what works for me. Hopefully, this works for you.

I've been reading different writing craft books, including The Artist's Way by Julia Cameron. She suggests "morning pages," where you write three pages daily for free. It's different from focusing on your project. It can be a chance to let go of what you're thinking about and dealing with in your life so you can later focus on your project. In other cases, it can be a place where you can motivate yourself to work on your project or even brainstorm ideas and what you will do for the next part of your project. She suggests it is each day, but she also points out that it's something you can work towards or revise to what works for you. This aspect can be useful for us to feel like we're making some writing process, even when we're struggling to find the right words on the page or not feeling as creative. It can also be a good way to deal with our stress and mental health. We need just as much space to deal with things; writing is one of the best ways. Having a different space to write but with lower pressure can give us the same feeling of making progress.

It's been tough for me lately as I've been struggling with my physical health, which also impacts my mental health. While working on it, some aspects can be tough because I could be doing more, but I don't have the energy to do so. I have constant reminders, including from our amazing writing community, to focus on resting and taking it easy. I'm trying to ensure that I do, but I'm figuring out when to write and read to make progress. Also, since I'm an indie author, I've got to do marketing and set everything up for standard formats to be published. Before the start of NaNoWriMo 2022, I had high hopes of progressing, but I've had to slow down. So what have I changed to make sure that I still make progress, but in a different way that works for me?

In the past year or so, I've been focused on writing an episode, editing, and publishing each week. Or at least as close as possible to each week. Along with keeping my readers updated on social media and my newsletter. Sometimes, I didn't feel right or didn't feel like I had the right setup yet to get it all done when I wanted to. It's been a learning curve to find a balance, not only between my work and writing but also with my health. I've had to be more compassionate and remind myself that it's okay that I didn't get what I wanted to be done and that readers will be willing to wait until I can publish more. I continue to work on this process. Most of all, it helps that you have a system set up for marketing so that you don't have to worry about it as much. After that, focus on trying to get something writing-related done per week. If you don't complete more on your project, you may have made some progress elsewhere. Some things readers won't see the process, and that might be something you want to share in case they are wondering where the next update is, but it's up to you. I try to let my readers know when I can.

Sometimes, you need a break from writing; this is when you can read a bit more similar or different work to what you are working on. This can really help you study the craft and experience writing from a different perspective. Sacha Black's book, The Anatomy of a Best Seller, provides a way for writers to read and study what they are reading to develop a way to learn from others about the writing craft. It's as easy as picking up a familiar or new story and noting what works and what you can see that you can improve. It's a helpful process for me, but also something familiar from my literary studies; while in college and grad school, it was about analyzing the text to understand it better. It's about using that analyzing skill to improve our writing craft. I hadn't seen a writing craft book in this way. It has inspired me in multiple ways, but it's a necessary process we can incorporate, especially when we're struggling to get words down.

Besides free writing, journaling during the week, planning out what you'll do, learning the craft, pondering away, and/or making some progress on your project, it's also important to value your mental health and physical health. Make sure you do what you can to care for yourself each day, including rest. We can only make progress if we take care of ourselves. Sometimes, it can be hard; we want to do so much, and some stuff is out of our control. Especially if you have chronic health issues, focus on what you can control. Learn about the writing craft (including reading), journal, brainstorm, plan, do some marketing, write when you can, and focus on what you can each week. Keep finding ways to move forward. Look for different ways and find what works for you. Once you continue to reflect each month and year, you'll see how much you've done, and it's more than you ever thought you would be able to. I know that is the case for me. I hope it is for you as well. We'll work on evaluating more later if you need it a bit more because even when you've got a learning curve, make sure you know how to pivot to find what can work for you when you need it the most.

EPISODE 10: REVALUATE WHAT YOU ARE DOING

Life doesn't go as you plan. I've learned that from experience. I worried about it, but I never would have really planned on getting lymphoma and dealing with chemotherapy. The side effects aren't as bad as I expected, especially after seeing the side effects of chemo on TV (as good as the TV show Chasing Life was). It's also a reminder that while storytelling is different, it can still be different for me as I'm experiencing something different from others who go through cancer and the chemo side effects. I know this from research. What does this have to do with writing and mental health, you might say? Well, one Chemo does sometimes affect my mental health as well. One of those pesky side effects. Also, because of how it drains me each round, I've had to learn to rest and step back in my writing and indie author career.

Sometimes, what worked for you a few months ago might not work for you today. My own experience is a good example. I was running on doing everything at over 100% at the beginning of 2022, even when I felt run down, likely from the lymphoma. As the year went on, I realized I couldn't keep up with that pace. It wasn't realistic for my health and everything that I do. While I still struggle with my mental health, I can't always rely on having a counselor every week. I've tried journaling, and it just wasn't working for me like it used to, even though it was suggested. I've noticed that others could write or journal while dealing with chemo. As a writer, I couldn't understand what was holding me back with my writing. Some of it, I've realized, is chemo brain. It's basically like brain fog, but different, as you have many more chemo effects to deal with, too. It took me some time to draw on my iPad mini and just post content on my social media to get to the point where I felt like I could take notes of what I wanted to do for this section and start writing.

It shows me and you that it's essential to do what you can with what you have. Another expressive art like digital drawing and coloring is sometimes necessary to switch to something different. Sometimes, even as writers, we can't express things with words, no matter how much we try. We can still express ourselves in some other way. I've seen how art therapy can be useful for children dealing with chemo, but I don't see it enough with adults. I think we need to remind ourselves that if we are dealing with chemo or not, we can't write. Find another creative outlet so you can still feel creative and express yourself. It allows us time to heal and the space to be able to write later. It doesn't have to be drawing; it can be photography, which I also enjoy but don't do enough as I would love to do. Remind me of that later. You can switch to nonfiction, as I do sometimes when I can't write creatively. You can creatively journal if you can. Or read something to enjoy and/or to study the craft.

When it comes to being an indie author, we're not only thinking about the writing we produce but also our presence online with our social media and newsletter; we have to rethink what we do here. That might be doing batch content, even if you don't want to, because you want to be as natural as possible online. I found what works a bit for me is thinking a week ahead. I noticed this week figuring out some posts I wanted to share and did it on Sunday when I was feeling better and ahead of my next round of Chemo. I noticed today that it made it easier for me to post and not worry about what I would do as much. This was a suggestion that has been given to me a few times in the past by several social media experts that I kept ignoring. I felt like it didn't feel natural enough. Some planned ones can be helpful, and some on the day you can. For example, I can make a drawing on my iPad that day and share it on my social media. Photography can be shared in the moment or later. It's all up to what you need at that moment and what you decide to share. Sometimes, you just can't post anything, and it's okay. Especially if you're dealing with chemo, remind me of this later. I think I'll need this reminder for the next chemo rounds.

Every new year, month, or period, I like to reflect on my progress and goals. Have I made progress? Not as much as I would like to. Why did you make that goal? It sounds like a resolution where someone decides to take one up and doesn't follow through. Well, that is why I do goals and not resolutions. Even if I don't complete the goal, I can complete it later. It might not be when I wanted it done, but there's no rush for me. Especially as many remind me, thank you, everyone, that my health is more important than worrying about my writing goals. Or even my part-time job. Or even updating a website. However, I keep doing many of these things because they matter to me. Even if it takes me more effort now than before or a bit different process than I'm used to, it's important to reflect to see what you can do a bit differently now but also to remind ourselves that we can't worry too much. We can reach what we hope to accomplish. We just have to find a different way of moving forward.

EPISODE 11: TAKE CARE OF YOUR HEALTH ALL OF IT

You might know this already, but I always want to do everything at 100 percent. I want to do my best in everything I need to do and want to do. I learned recently that I've had performance anxiety that has affected me since childhood. The first time I created art to present to others (besides my parents and my family) was in elementary school, especially when I was in a dance school. This school had recitals every year. I wanted to do my best and worried about making a mistake. So, I would check the side of the theater stage for my teacher, who was reminding us of the dance steps. It was like the training wheels for a bike. However, this analogy isn't good since I never learned how to ride a bike after removing the training wheels. Or maybe it is a good analogy. I feared making a mistake in both situations, but one would more likely hurt me physically. We have anxiety in many cases to help protect us from harm, but in many cases, that anxiety could be the fear holding us back from our true potential. This performance anxiety has not only held me back more than I've realized, but it has led me to add more pressure on myself to make what matters to me as perfect as possible, in many cases, my writing.

For good reason, we are drawn to write as best as possible. This isn't for perfection or awards but to make sure people can read what we are writing as best as they can. In many cases, this pressure has led to us holding back from what we could do. Sometimes, we do not get the opportunities we deserve because we feel like our writing isn't good enough, even if we edit it and/ or have help editing it. We can sometimes not believe that our work is good enough when people tell us it is because we have read reviews that tell us otherwise. Some authors have decided not to look at reviews or have someone else look at them. If they have someone look at them, that person can decide which ones the author can receive to read and share with others. While I like this idea, it can lead us to believe that our work is always perfect. Sometimes, we do need to see critical reviews to improve. At the same time, it can hurt us to see a one-star review, especially if it says bad things about you personally more than your writing. We're also reminded that reviews are for readers as well. So, where do we fit when it comes to reviews? Just like with our writing, we have to find a way to find what works for us and our mental health. Yes, reviews do affect our mental health.

As writers, we must find a balance to continue to share our work with others and not be held back by reviews, especially since they are subjective in many cases. Everyone has their own opinion on what they think, especially what they think is good writing. I had really strong side effects from Chemo recently that caused me to go to the hospital. I'm doing better now. I still have a bit more chemotherapy to go. This scared me even more than my average anxiety. I thought I could balance what affected me as a writer and everything I did outside of being an indie author. Even though I knew I needed to care for myself and my mental health, I still needed more help. This is okay. As Priscilla Oliveras has said (on social media), "What matters is making progress on your project in whatever process works for you." I knew that, but I continue to need that reminder. We sometimes have to slow down what we want to do and make our goals a bit different to help us get there eventually. For example, find a time each week or month to complete some writing instead of writing each day. You are making progress, but it might take longer than expected. It's something I continue to work on. It's hard. I have different things that I do and want to do.

In this time of struggle, I not only had a change of plans for my book release of 'Never Forget' (I had plans to post something each day online to promote the release and didn't get a chance to do it all), but I also realized what was holding me back was more than just performance anxiety. I had my generational trauma that I had to deal with and understand. I had anxiety, lack of communication, and difficulty dealing with grief passed down unintentionally, along with my grandmother's unintentional lymphoma. It was all affecting me physically, mentally, and emotionally. I feared death, even though I believe in an afterlife from my faith, which has led to me struggling with sleeping, but my anxiety also kept me thinking and worrying late at night. That lack of sleep was affecting my health in all forms. I couldn't be at my best until I got the help I needed from medical, psychological, and personal. As soon as I started to address what had been affecting me, I started to see that I was feeling better. Not 100 percent. I still need to finish fighting lymphoma (a blood cancer), but I feel hopeful and better about my chances and what I can do in different aspects of my life.

It also dawned on me that generational trauma was the real focus of my writing from Latinx Romance, poetry, and craft writing. I have a better idea of how I can promote my writing and continue my writing moving forward because I know what I need to instruct, inspire, and engage in making my social media and my writing the best it can be to continue to share what I write and more people will know what I write about. We are seeing more generational trauma being featured in stories because we are finally trying to address it. We can move toward a better future once we can see, experience, and find ways to change things. This works also in poetry because we can address our mental health by expressing our thoughts in poetry form. In craft writing, I'm addressing different forms of dealing with mental health and making strides in our writing. It's all connected, but it took me a while for me to realize it; even in my struggles, I found something worthwhile. That is a good reminder for all of us. We can find something good even when we struggle. Nothing can be perfect, and when we realize that, we can free ourselves to share ourselves with the world the best way we can through our writing.

I also realized that I was holding myself back in a different way. I didn't want to admit that I was a self-published author as an indie author. We still have a stigma on mental health in many areas and with self-pub and indie authors. Since I'm both, I wanted people to think I needed to improve. So, I have yet to promote as much that I'm a self-published author while being an independent author. There's nothing wrong with this path. We are doing something really risky. We're sharing our writing as best as possible with the funding to make our writing available to others. We are still determining how it will work out. We're putting so much into our work with little in return, but that isn't what matters the most; it's that we have the chance to make a difference to our readers, no matter how many they are. If someone has read our work, we're successful. It can be hard to see it that way when we're told we must be best-selling or make a lot of money to succeed. Even those authors are still determining if they truly have success; it's really up to how the readers respond. It's something that has led me to be thankful that I've gone the self-pub, indie author path. Suppose I had pushed myself to follow what some suggested to stick to traditional publishing. I would probably still be waiting and wondering if my writing was good enough. Now I know that people are reading, even if it takes time, and finding something worthwhile with my writing. It wouldn't have happened if I didn't take that risk. So, I wasn't holding myself back too much. What I can do moving forward will continue to make me a better writer.

EPISODE 12: SMALL FLEXIBLE STEPS AND EXPRESSIVE SELF-CARE

Every April, poets worldwide participate in the challenge to write poems, and many of them 30 poems in 30 days. I'm one of them. Did you know that poetry isn't just another form of writing? It can be a way to improve one's mental health. Realistically, any kind of writing, especially creative, can provide this. There's something special about poetry, including expressive writing. When we think of expressive writing, we think of journaling, personal essay writing, and memoirs. It's also poetry too. But not all poetry is about expressing oneself. It can be from different perspectives from the poet or even fiction in verse. How does expressive writing, especially poetry, bring value to our mental health no matter what we struggle with?

Talking about traumatic events, stressful situations, and about ourselves is part of a natural human response. Through writing, we can experience this more freely because, in many cases, we do not see our readers. We have a space to ponder our thoughts and think about what we will say, even go back and improve our writing to make it clearer for ourselves and eventually for readers. When starting, it's best to be able not to let how the reader will perceive our writing but allow the flow of thought onto the page so nothing will impact the raw essence of what will come forward. This is something that can also be done with poetry if we let it. Not let the words held back from being told because of what others have said. Being free to write in the beginning helps our mental health by letting our minds process what has happened without judgment.

We often take notes of our thoughts in journaling to clear our minds. There might be a lot on our minds that we are trying to deal with, and putting it down allows us not to worry about forgetting something we're doing or working on. This can be a factor in some anxiety. Doing this process with journaling or being creative, like poetry, can also provide a way to visually find solutions to resolve the issues we're dwelling on. If we can also write down the information we want to remember, we can give our mind space to focus on other aspects. Additionally, we can promote more writing when we free-write or note down what we want to write.

As readers, reading allows us to think about the world around us and see things from different perspectives when we allow ourselves to read diversely. As writers, writing allows us to explore and even change how we think about the world with the hope of a better outcome. There are even some studies that explore the way expressive writing impacts mental health, especially among cancer patients. It doesn't cure the disease but helps people adjust to the changes daily. Writing can enhance different processes, such as emotional, behavioral, and psychological. Anything that influences the mind also influences the body. This could be a way that writing improves overall health and well-being.

If we see the different forms of expressive writing, we can also view how they can impact together. Journaling is the freeform start. The personal essay, or the longer-form memoir, is more organized, and poetry is artistically organized even in its freeform state. It's really up to us as writers how we want to use them. It can be a way for us to express ourselves even if it isn't what we would eventually publish. Or it can springboard something that we might want to publish someday. The most crucial part is that it holds value to you first.

Even with these ways of expressing ourselves, we might still find some aspects daunting. That's why it's essential to have some flexibility in our habits, and the more we make those habits when we can, they can lead towards what we hope to accomplish, aka our goals. Having the flexibility of choosing a small, medium, or large habit allows us to focus on progress and consistency more than focusing on something that might be harder to obtain with our current limits. This can help our mental health by not allowing the stress of high expectations to restrict us from making a small step forward. Reaching a goal, especially a big one, can be fantastic, but it can also be stressful if you place the goal when your body (including your mind) isn't ready for it.

It's something that I've realized recently as I've recovered from chemotherapy. While writing has helped me to have something to keep striving for, it can be stressful when my body has been affected by the chemo and not in its standard form. That's why I quickly question advice suggesting people should push forward and write even if they feel they can't. While I understand there are deadlines, providing a flexible step forward can help us feel like we are making progress while allowing our bodies the rest to be able to provide more later. It can explain why I was frustrated at the beginning of my healing journey. I wanted to write still like I usually did or express myself in some way in writing. I was putting too much pressure when things were changing. While things are much better now, I'm still in recovery.

As much as I want to reach 30 poems in 30 days, I'm still determining if I will be able to this year, even though I know I've done it before in previous years. Even in some cases, I've caught up during the month to reach the goal. I could still catch up, but I must also focus on my main goal: healing. If I focus on flexible goals, I need to do one or two when possible versus trying to do as many poems as possible to catch up to the latest day. It also can apply to other aspects of my indie author career. If I can't share a book marketing post like I want, I could share someone else's. If I can't read something that day, I have to find something else I can read or keep the reading to something small. That way, I can do what I want to do each day while also realizing that I have to have the energy to do things that I need to do. This is also where additional self-care can help to bring energy for the day or at least recharge when needed.

It's all easier said than done. It's something to ponder about. As well as to try and see if it works for you. As long as you give yourself some time. You will see progress later. I'm just as impatient as a kid waking up early on Christmas morning, but even I must remind myself. Let's work together on it.

EPISODE 13:
DON'T LET HIGH EXPECTATIONS BRING YOU DOWN

As writers, we can have many expectations from others and ourselves. I've been told from time to time that I'm a perfectionist. It's never rooted in wanting to be perfect but being my best. Some of it is also rooted in generational expectations, especially as the only daughter with many cousins. I knew I needed to do my best in school and later at work. There was no question about it, and I have always wanted that. That desire to be the best that I can be can become a stressor in making progress. How can you feel confident about your work when you don't know what your "best" can be? It's tough because everyone has their idea of what that can be.

Growing up, my best was ensuring I did well in reading and writing. So people wouldn't notice that having two languages was negative. Now, having more than one language is a positive in many ways. There was always a concern because, as soon as I started school, they knew that I spoke more than one language at home. They needed to find out if I could excel in English. This changed over time, especially when I didn't want to speak up in class. It's always been something that has made me wonder about how well I could speak, read, and write. I even had teachers and professors that have made me question my writing ability. Thankfully, I had many other teachers and professors who inspired me to follow my passions for writing and reading.

All these pressures I knew led me to have high expectations, especially about productivity. Especially around others, including supervisors, who expected much from me. It's understandable in many cases, but it's also no wonder why I questioned whether I was "good enough." Even later, through publishing, I had doubts when it seemed that certain people (like agents and editors) weren't willing to help in traditional publishing. Even when I grew confident that self-publishing as an indie author was the right path for me, it's still looming, with a few reviews suggesting that my writing isn't up to par.

Even the people willing to support me in editing often need more time, or it might cost too much for quality service. So, I have had to decide where to be confident right now and build from there. That can help all writers. We all have strengths that we know we have. That's a good starting point. We're always constantly learning. It's helpful to remind ourselves about that. We all have the opportunity to improve. We must simplify what we do in everyday writing life so it can be manageable. Don't focus on perfect results. We have to focus on progress and consistency.

Lately, I have yet to be able to get enough writing done. I always compare it to what I could do before I started fighting lymphoma. Other times, I compare it to how much I should be doing to attract more readers and sales or reads. Every time I do, I keep reminding myself that I have made some progress from writing more poetry, writing this nonfiction, and being consistent in my social media and newsletter presence. I know those are strides forward. As I continue making small strides forward, I will make gains toward what I want to accomplish and improve everything I'm doing as an indie author.

Focus on caring about making progress in some way and how you can make that happen. I've learned with elastic habits that I'm changing how I view being consistent. If I can't do one thing, I have another option that might be smaller or feel more doable to complete for the day. So with that, you can still win. We can enjoy the process when we start with progress (and not aim for success) and accept it in any size. So we need to remember what is holding us back (in my case, my health, physical and mental) and focus on what we can do. That way, we start where we

most important per day, week, and month. A little bit per day or week can add up. Check off what you've completed and celebrate the small wins. I use a calendar to write down and check off things. If I can't finish something, I make an arrow through it to move it to another day. We could create a self-care emergency kit where you place what you think will help you most when needed. When we have that setup, it can help us get through our priority list.

No matter what we try to add to our priority list, we have to be kind to ourselves and add rest breaks. It won't help if you consistently focus the most on writing without refilling the well. Even when it comes to writing, there are other things you can do that can count, such as reading or experiencing different kinds of entertainment. This focus on your priorities allows you to take some control of your journey. Especially when times going through health aspects feels impossible. It can also help set up certain things you don't have to worry about as much. Stay simple with marketing your work, giving more time for writing and reading.

Even when you know your priority, it still takes time to make progress and see that progress. We can reflect when we can, as often as possible, to remind ourselves what progress we are making and ensure our priorities are still in line. It might help to prioritize short time, short writing amounts, and comfort while writing. It doesn't help to have your priorities be something that will add more stress instead of making writing the passion that it is meant to be. A lot of this is what works for you. Only you know what brings you comfort while you write, like you know what amount short is for your writing sessions. Will this make you finish quickly on your projects? It might, but that should be something other than what should be your focus.

It can be hard to know what writing will work out for others, including this one. I try my best to write what others will find valuable, but it also has to be something I'm drawn to write. That's my priority, but I try to find what I can do afterward. Sometimes, it can be something small like writing a poem for the day (or two) or completing a nonfiction section (once a month at least) that allows me to express my process and thoughts. It can be journaling (including art), note-taking, and making plans (including on a calendar or lists). I still need to figure out what small steps I can take toward fiction writing. That's now on my priority list.

Don't let your priorities, plans, or other things you want to do become something that stresses you. It's easier said than done. Even I can have that unintentional habit of feeling like I'm not doing enough if I don't reach a certain amount of my writing each month. It helps that I'm aware of it. When we are aware of it, we can make sure that it's still something important, but it's also time to figure out how to reset our minds about it. We can accomplish more than we can even imagine. Or provide ourselves with the rest that we desperately need.

No matter how hard that rest might take to happen. Life only allows us a few opportunities to focus on rest, and when we do, it's something we are used to doing if it's a trip to enjoy things to do. So we must prioritize even figuring out what will allow us to rest and revitalize for our next steps. When we prioritize what matters, we might realize that we can also find ways to take risks that will benefit us in ways we may not even realize. Let's reflect, brainstorm, plan, and ultimately reset through rest.

As we move forward, we can find what will work for us and our writing. Then, repeat as often as needed. Our bodies (and minds) know when we need to organize differently; we just have to be open to taking notice of those signs. Also, remember to do those necessary things, like getting the right food and water. If not, it might slip us by and make things worse.

EPISODE 15: TAKE RISKS WHEN IT MATTERS

Becoming a writer who will share your work with others is a risk. Many of us would say it is a risk worth taking. Bringing this forward is essential because it's connected to everything we do in our writing careers and how we care for ourselves. As I've mentioned often, I bring advice that I must remind myself to take because I add more pressure to myself and everything I do. It's important to know that when you read and move forward. As writers, we always wonder if our path will work and how things will turn out. That is part of the risk. If we don't take the chance, we won't know how much our writing can impact, but it also allows additional growth to write with the audience in mind.

After that big step, whether publishing your first book or getting started in a writing job, we continue to take risks with new stories or new projects that we do, along with how we make that writing happen and make it available and aware to others. Even in the writing process, something different can feel like a risk because we are still determining if it will work or if the process will be better. Also, taking breaks, pacing, and doing self-care can be risks because we don't know how much time will help and how much time away can impact, but it is needed. The culture of productivity and lack of money earned for our work can cause many of us to burnout. Once we get there, finding the way out of that situation can be challenging.

I bring this up from my perspective as an indie author. Taking the step to self-publish my work through Kindle Vella and eventually through Amazon's Kindle Direct Publishing was after looking at the traditional path and focusing on what I wanted through publishing. While traditional publishing has its benefits, I wanted to be able to make the decisions, even if they will sometimes make me little money. I want my writing to be available, and more people will be interested as I continue to market my work. With more interest, I can invest more towards having more help editing my work. I also need to make more money to be full-time as a writer. So, I have a part-time job to help me, but it can be a risk, too. In this case, it can add more stress or decrease my energy towards the time I could have for writing and eventually publishing. This is why I continue to work on figuring out a good balance.

I've learned to take risks from Jeremy Jordan (actor, singer, and songwriter from Corpus Christi, Texas). He has inspired me in different ways, but two important ones are to take care of my mental health and find a way to make sure what matters most becomes my priority (for example, my indie author career). He has talked about taking risks when auditioning for roles and eventually deciding what work will be best for him. But his latest risk has been to make his songwriting available through his indie band Age of Madness with concerts and selling music. He has had to learn how to make things possible with his band, just as I have figured out how to be an indie author. Now he has a leg up since he already had fans from being an actor and a singer, but he has admitted in interviews that it still takes effort because only some of his fans will be interested in his rock music.

This is a good reminder. Our writing will only apply to some. So we have to focus our efforts on those who will be interested. Throughout the year, we must reflect and figure out when to take a risk. This might differ per person and situation. Journaling about what you could do to keep moving forward can help. It can be a good visual to look at later when needed. Additionally, maybe in that journal, remember the "why" you write and use that to push forward. It helps when you need more sales or reach a specific goal. One of the ways you can also incorporate risk can be incorporating fun, even if that takes you away from what plans you originally had.

I have been writing poetry and getting back into fiction writing. While I am making progress with my poetry writing, I need to catch up on fiction writing. I changed that by writing a little bit for fun; I started working on plans for a TV spec feature script. While it is unlikely ever to become something for TV, it gives me good practice for writing, especially something new. Plus, TV writing also helped inspire my last fictional book, NEVER FORGET, as I originally started the story as a TV pilot original. It worked so well through the Kindle Vella serial platform, as it was released a bit at a time like a TV series.

The point I'm trying to make is that while this might be seen as "procrastination" since I'm not doing what I had initially planned for my indie work, it actually benefits me more than just writing practice. It reminds me that I can find joy in writing and reminds me why I write in the first place. While I'm still working on writing that TV script, I can always go back to writing a bit more later, but the goal of it makes it worth my time. As much as we know that we must be making progress to complete our goals, we must let go of productivity guilt. I know that I will continue to do so. It's one of the best ways to move forward. We might feel that any time off from our planned projects will not be fruitful, but that's all from the productivity guilt that makes us feel like any time off is "lazy."

There are even risks in recovery. For me, beyond my mental health, at this moment, I'm still recovering from fighting lymphoma and winning. No matter how much I plan and figure out what I want to do, my body has limits I don't know each day. I have to work with that all the time. Every decision feels like a risk. If I do more, it will affect my body worse. If I do less, I'll be behind on something and have issues with my part-time job. I know now from my fight with lymphoma that it matters to take care of my health., along with providing opportunities to enjoy life, including when I'm writing. Are you willing to take a risk toward your goals and, most of all, your mental and overall health?

EPISODE 16: THE FUTURE IS A LEARNING CURVE

We will never know what the future holds. I might write another nonfiction like this in the future explaining those things, but I still need to find out what is ahead. Since I can't predict the future, all we can do is figure out what strategies might help us handle what the future gives us. I still need to figure out how to get what I need and want done while prioritizing my health, including rest.

This is part of my recovery from fighting lymphoma. I still feel side effects from the lymphoma treatment and will likely continue for at least a few more months. Even then, I still need to make sure I take things easy because it's pretty like those dealing with chronic fatigue (where there is no specific cause); if I push myself too much, I can crash and struggle much more later. So it's all about pacing, beyond writing, of course. I know not everyone is dealing with that. So, you must find a pace that will work for you and what you are dealing with.

We have to learn not only from our exploration but also from others. I recently learned it will help me incorporate more storytelling into my newsletter on social media. You might say? How can someone who writes not be doing enough storytelling? While some aspects might work for others, such as focusing on specific tropes or hooks to bring interest to the reader, it might not work for me and my published work. It gives a bit of what my work is about, but since I'm an indie author, it's more important for readers to know who I am and why I am writing through storytelling so I can give them a reason to get interested in my stories and poems.

Besides that, I found it helpful to narrow my social media posts to three main weekly updates, just like when I narrowed down my newsletter from weekly to monthly. It allows me to create content worth keeping track of versus posting to attract interest. This should also give me more time and energy to focus on my writing, which is even more critical because I'm still recovering and trying to care for myself alongside different priorities beyond my indie career. Incorporating some of this aspect might work for your process, too, especially if you're an indie writer.

Beyond this, I will continue to learn the writing craft through workshops, reading, and mental health strategies through counseling and additional reading. I will continue learning about book marketing and how to incorporate aspects of self-care into that. I will continue to focus on diverse stories and supporting diverse writers. I will learn more about my cultures and how to incorporate them more into my writing. After my current projects, I will have to figure out what to do next. It's a lot to focus on, but taking it bit by bit while making a list that I can check off as I go on will help.

Even with all those things in mind, I still need to figure out my long-term goals. I plan to publish more fiction, poetry, and nonfiction. I know I can do it. It's really figuring out how to progress to complete the projects. While I want to keep publishing through Kindle Vella, I will surely continue publishing through standard formats. We can worry a lot about what will happen, significantly, as indie writers, but it won't help us. We just need to keep learning and finding ways to share our writing.

That sounds good, but what about emerging technology? I enjoy tech, but we must ensure it's only used as a tool, not a replacement for human quality. We must support some technology that helps us while showing our value as writers. Anything that causes us to cheat the system is only for profit; it will not ultimately help you or our community. The value of our work should outshine. It's something that the current 2023 writers' strike is fighting for, along with making sure they are being paid fairly.

Also, looking at the value of our work is connected to the idea of creating writing that matters versus stressing out in the process of producing a lot. I'm not saying that producing a lot is bad because many can do it, but if it starts to affect you negatively, is it worth it? How can you keep writing if you feel burned out? It's easy to say, but it can be challenging for many who don't have a lot of money, and being able to write more can help. We have to find some kind of balance. That can be focusing more on fun and less on productivity, which can be tough. I know from my own experience. We also have to focus on preventing burnout in the future, no matter what situation we might have.

In Supergirl's TV show episode, Winn Schott was heading to the future (literally to the 31st century). Sorry for the spoiler if you haven't seen it, but in a particular scene, he says that "the future will be a steep learning curve" slightly as a joke but also because he notices that the future tech isn't familiar to him. He will have to learn a lot to reach the level he needs to work with the technology. While it's apparent that he's one of my top favorite characters for many reasons, I find the words come to me when I struggle with something tech-related but mainly something new. It also works for what I'm discussing here and what I hope we continue to consider moving forward. We need to know that not knowing what is ahead will be tough, but if we're ready to learn, we can succeed.

EPISODE 17: TEAMWORK MAKES THE DREAM WORK

Here we are at the end of this nonfiction book. The final chapter's title is another quote from Winn Schott, even though it's a common saying. It has always stood out to me since he has said it. It means a lot in the TV show Supergirl, especially since working together as a team allows for much of the character Supergirl's success. However, I found it essential because I've always found help with others to work towards my notable goals.

It was really noticeable as I started my indie author career. In every step, I've had people willing to help me by providing feedback for improvement and support as I release my writing in publishing. While this can be common in our wonderful community, it isn't always. We need to work on that to help more in our writing community, especially those who don't have as many advantages. Besides that, I continue to be thankful for the support that I have received, especially during my lymphoma fight.

When I found out early on, fellow writers came to let me know they were thinking of me and willing to support me in what they could do. One noticeable thing was when a group of writers I've known and called friends made a notebook with messages, including purchasing a video of an actress from Supergirl, who also stars in the Hallmark channel, Andrea Brooks. She sent a wonderful video message of support. Besides that, another act of support would be reading my published work and sharing about it when they could. I'm so thankful to have many in the writing community and beyond supporting me throughout my indie author career, especially when I struggled. While I still feel like I'm recovering, I continue to receive support in taking care of myself and supporting me as I progress towards my new publishing goals.

In this process, I've realized how important it is to have a team belong to. It's a reminder that we must keep supporting each other unless something needs to be critiqued. Not only during a difficult time but always. I'm thankful to those who have inspired me, including fellow writers. I'm thankful to those who read my work, including writers. I want to add beyond working together to help each other., we should also reflect on and thank everyone we can. It makes a difference more than we can ever imagine.

As an indie author, I do a lot on my own. I want more people to be aware of that for us indie authors, but we also have a lot of people who help us and make a difference in each step of our careers. Now that the TV writers' strike has concluded and won, they were successful because they worked together as a team and were supported by so many, including fellow writers in other areas. There is still much work to be done for them, but they finally made progress towards helping writers be seen as valuable. While there is a strike for the actors working towards their fair deal that we should support, it's a constant reminder that we can make strides if we can see where we can help each other.

Let's remember the important points: we should take care of ourselves, not pressure ourselves as much, and help support each other. We can continue to help upcoming published authors or writers starting in their careers because it benefits us all.

BOOKS BY THIS AUTHOR

Liberty Calling

Of all the comic book shops in South Texas, Lola Cortes (Mexican immigrant) walked into his. Chase Benitez learns of their newborn daughter, Evita, when Lola is taken from the hospital by ICE.

Chase needs to overcome family dynamics to renunite with his new family. But will Lola find the hero within before Chase finds where she is? It is within reach when systematic obstacles get in their way.

Years later, Evita's parents' story leads her to stardom, but when she is drawn back home, she realizes that every version of love matters.

In a time when life feels uncertain, Liberty Calling will be an emotional journey with a guaranteed hopeful ending. It's the perfect time to buy this debut, a stand-alone in an interconnected series.

Never Forget

Would you join a psychological study to pay for college?

Valencia Calderon never expected her college would be paid for through a study that dealt with her trauma of losing her parents before high school graduation.

The study's tech wizard, Xavier Gomez, is the only one she trusts and gets closer to since her best friend, Jasmine Dias, recently moved away and is difficult to reach.

As we join Valencia through the study, we begin to learn along with her, especially the study's layers: who's working, running, and created it? It's up to Valenica to write her destiny through the past.

Never Forget will be an interesting mystery to delve into with an inspiring ending. It's the right time to buy this second stand-alone book in an interconnected series.

Write From The Heart, Edit With Precise Measure (A Poetry & Short Story Collection)

Get a taste of Christina Vourcos' writing through this collection. She takes to heart about being compassionate as she delves into different topics before and after the COVID-19 pandemic. Precise Measure doesn't mean perfection, but taking what she has and making it into something worthwhile.

Over several years, Christina Vourcos has been inspired to write 30 poems in 30 days during the poetry community's challenge NaPoWriMo (National Poetry Writing Month every year in April). Many were first written through her blog each day as she was inspired by a prompt or something that she was drawn to. After some time, she believed that the poems would be better read through standard publishing. So she collected these poems along with poems written in the past and added three short stories inspired by two of her friends and her Greek culture. Throughout her poetry, she blends her Greek, Latinx, and Hispanic cultures, along with some nerd references. This is her first poetry and short story collection.

Christina Vourcos is currently working on her next poetry book which will be more focused, with poems on her fight with lymphoma, mental health, and recover along with a novella-in-verse of characters dealing with mental health.

ABOUT THE AUTHOR

Christina Vourcos

 She writes what matters in Latinx Romance and beyond. As a Greek Latina, she is inspired by both of her cultures but feels that Latinx allows her to be more diverse. There are some connections to her Greek heritage and hopes to add a bit more, but her Latinx heritage is something that isn't focused on enough in many mediums. She is bilingual with Spanish and wants to be trilingual in Greek. She enjoys making nerd references in her writing. From fiction to non-fiction, books, Kindle Vella serials, short stories, and poetry, she does it all as best as she can.

Made in the USA
Coppell, TX
08 November 2023

23956419R00039